INSPIRE
HAIR FASHION FOR SALON CLIENTS

Primary Syn HAIR: Johnny COLOR: Annette Abdelfatah PHOTO: Johnathon Roe

INSPIRE

HAIR FASHION FOR SALON CLIENTS

Featuring Men, Women & Children

Table of Contents Volume 65

Salon Coccolé
HAIR: Salon Coccolé
COLOR: Salon Coccolé
MAKE-UP: Salon Coccolé
PHOTO: Salon Coccolé

Studio C Salon- Irvine, CA
HAIR: Shaun Chapman
MAKE-UP: Cosmo
PHOTO: Taggart Winterhalter
for Purely Visual

Crème Colour Lounge
HAIR: Whitney Sears
MAKE-UP: Jaime Queenin
PHOTO: Taggart Winterhalter for Purely Visual

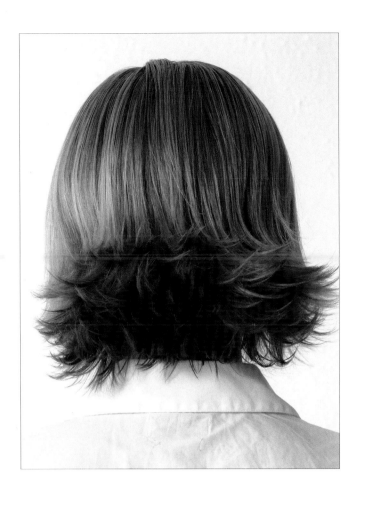

Somers Salon & Spa
HAIR: April Wurtsthorne
MAKE-UP: Amanda Kelley
PHOTO: Dianne Paulson

Studio C Salon- Irvine, CA
HAIR: Daniella Faubion
MAKE-UP: Daniella Faubion
PHOTO: Taggart Winterhalter
for Purely Visual

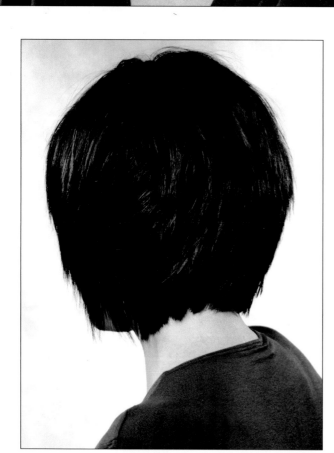

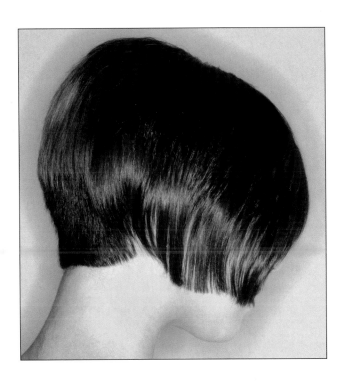

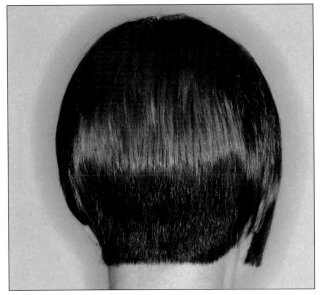

Vincent Michael Salon
HAIR: Vincent Michael for ENJOY
MAKE-UP: Sara Wayne
PHOTO: Taggart Winterhalter
for Purely Visual

Evolution Spa
HAIR: Hannah Park
MAKE-UP: Hannah Park
PHOTO: Karl Nakamura

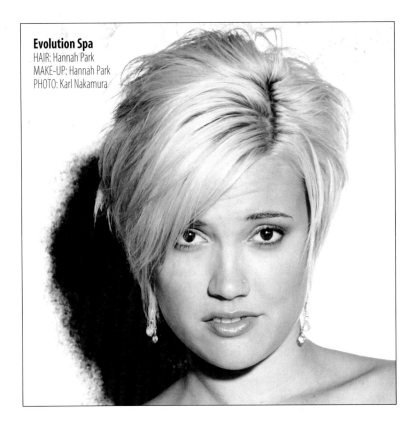

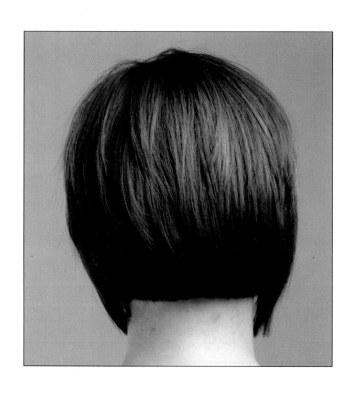

Avant Gard Hair Salon
HAIR: Brooke Rhea
COLOR: Brooke Rhea
MAKE-UP: Lacey Walker
PHOTO: Scott Bryant
Art Direction by Larry Oskin &
The Marketing Solutions Team

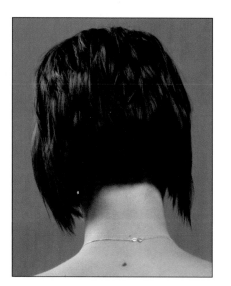

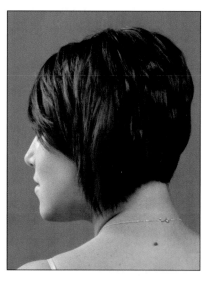

**Avant Gard
Hair Salon**
HAIR: Kristen Corn
COLOR: Kristen Corn
MAKE-UP: Angela Minnick
PHOTO: Scott Bryant
Art Direction by Larry Oskin &
The Marketing Solutions Team

8

HAIR:Damien Carney
PHOTO:Hama Sanders
*Courtesy of NAHA

élon Salon-Marietta, GA
HAIR: Don Westbrook
COLOR: Don Westbrook
MAKE-UP: Fawn/Mac
PHOTO: Scott Bryant
Art Direction by Larry Oskin &
The Marketing Solutions Team

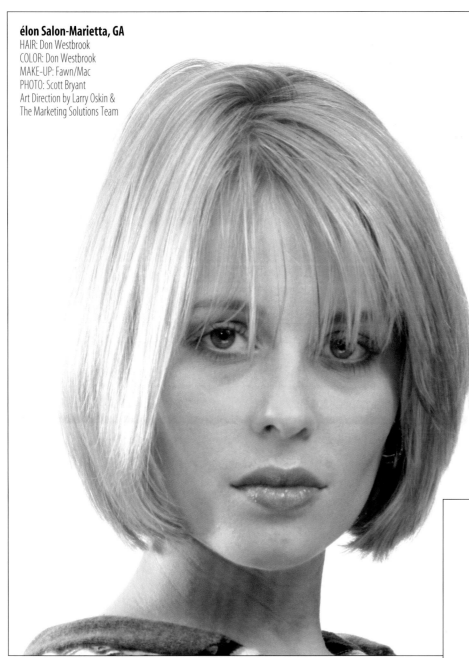

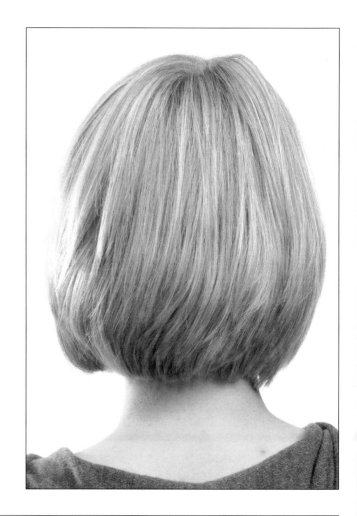

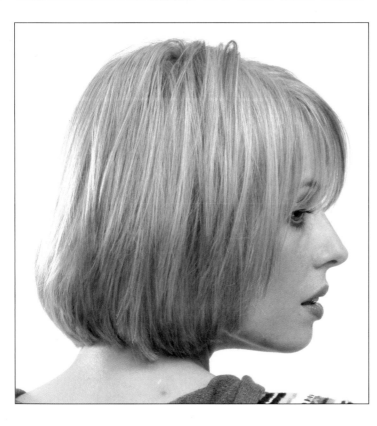

Diadema Hair Fashion
HAIR: Diadema
MAKE-UP: 20100Milano
PHOTO: Stefano Bidini

Diadema Hair Fashion
HAIR: I Fuoriclasse
MAKE-UP: 20100Milano
PHOTO: Stefano Bidini

Salon Boucle
HAIR: Mehran
MAKE-UP: Sara Wayne
PHOTO: Taggart Winterhalter
for Purely Visual

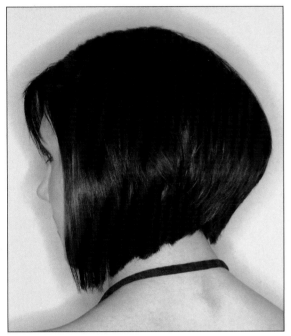

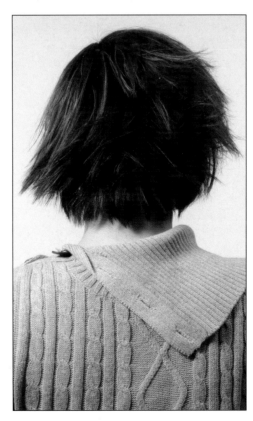

**Hair Benders Internationale-
Chattanooga, TN**
HAIR: Hair Benders Design Team
COLOR: Hair Benders Design Team
MAKE-UP: Darin Wright
PHOTO: Scott Bryant
Art Direction by Larry Oskin &
The Marketing Solutions Team

13

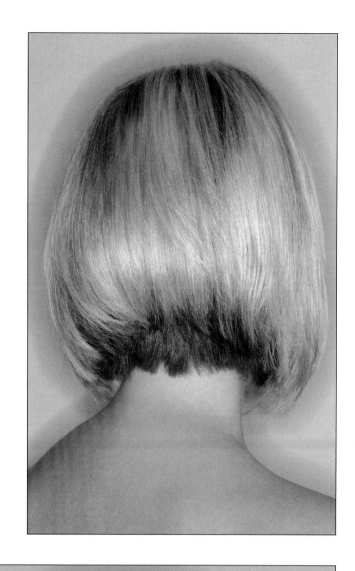

Art of Hair
HAIR: Nicole Martin
MAKE-UP: Sara Wayne
PHOTO: Taggart Winterhalter
for Purely Visual

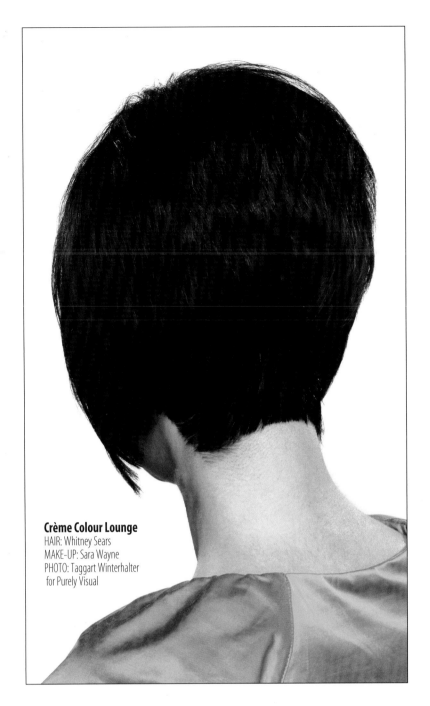

Crème Colour Lounge
HAIR: Whitney Sears
MAKE-UP: Sara Wayne
PHOTO: Taggart Winterhalter
 for Purely Visual

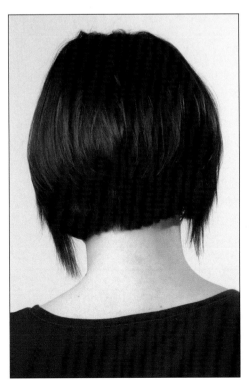

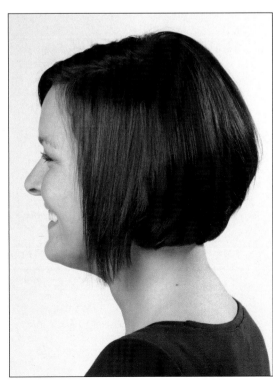

**Avant Gard
Hair Salon**
HAIR: Kristen Corn
COLOR: Kristen Corn
MAKE-UP: Kristen Corn
PHOTO: Scott Bryant
Art Direction by Larry Oskin &
The Marketing Solutions Team

15

The Art of Hair Salon
HAIR: Jennifer Oakley
MAKE-UP: Marcia Brazona
PHOTO: Ray Lansky

Planet Salon-Lexington, KY
HAIR: Ashley Umstead
MAKE-UP: Ashley Umstead
PHOTO: Jeff Rogers

Trendsets
HAIR: Jordan Hope
PHOTO: Robert Holmes,
Shooting Stars

e'lon Salon-Marietta, GA
HAIR: Dee Dee Hightower
COLOR: Dee Dee Hightower
MAKE-UP: Nico
PHOTO: Scott Bryant
Art Direction by Larry Oskin &
The Marketing Solutions Team

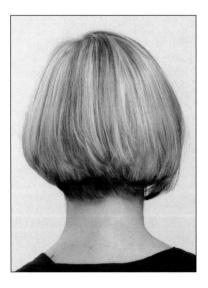

**John Amico Haircare
& Jalyd Haircolor**
HAIR: Yenz & Reinout Von Tilborg
COLOR: Yenz & Reinout Von Tilborg
MAKE-UP: Yenz & Reinout Von Tilborg
PHOTO: Scott Bryant
Art Direction by Larry Oskin & The Marketing Solutions Team

Pivot Point International
HAIR: Zo (Yi Chen) Tsai-Pivot Point Tiawan
MAKE-UP: Dino
PHOTO: Mike van den Toorn/Tina Rayyan

Coiffeur XYZ Createur
HAIR: Michael Del Bronco for XYZ
COLOR: Sylvie Hendrikx et Maryline Forges
MAKE-UP: Juan Pacifico
PHOTO: Evelyne De Mey@BG project

Crème Colour Lounge
HAIR: Amanda Ryan
MAKE-UP: Sara Wayne
PHOTO: Taggart Winterhalter
for Purely Visual

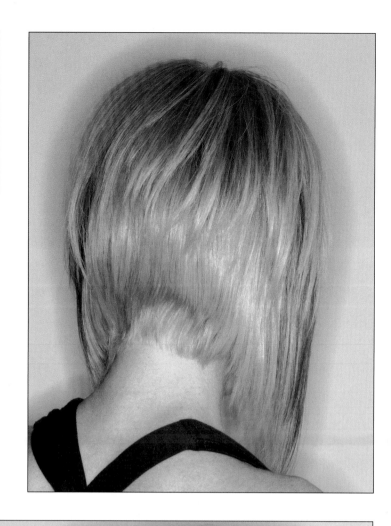

Aveda Frederic's Institute
HAIR: Jessica Zehnder
PHOTO: Babak
*Courtesy of NAHA

Somers Salon & Spa
HAIR: Jill Somers
MAKE-UP: Amanda Kelley
PHOTO: Dianne Paulson

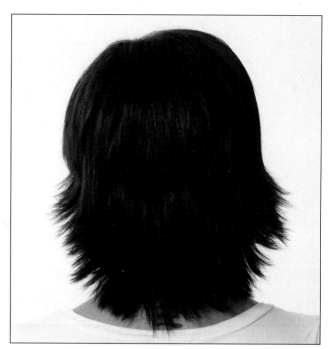

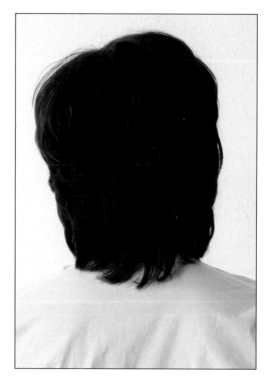

Tantrum Salon
HAIR: Hector Lopez
MAKE-UP: Sara Wayne
PHOTO: Taggart Winterhalter
for Purely Visual

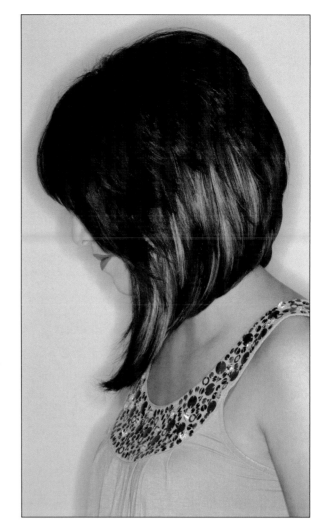

**Advanced
College of
Cosmotology**
HAIR: Advanced
College of Cosmotology
MAKE-UP: Advanced
College of Cosmotology
PHOTO: Doug Raflik

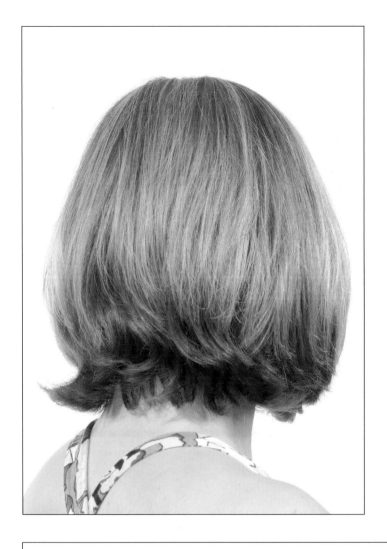

élon Salon-Marietta, GA
HAIR: Nancy Jones
COLOR: Nancy Jones
MAKE-UP: Nico
PHOTO: Scott Bryant

élon Salon-Marietta, GA
HAIR: Don Westbrook
COLOR: Don Westbrook
MAKE-UP: Fawn/Mac
PHOTO: Scott Bryant
Art Direction by
Larry Oskin
& The Marketing
Solutions Team

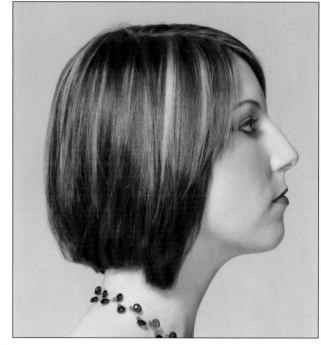

Hair Benders Internationalé-Chattanooga, TN
HAIR: Hair Benders Internationale
COLOR: Hair Benders Internationale
MAKE-UP: Bray Martin
PHOTO: Scott Bryant
Art Direction by Larry Oskin
& The Marketing Solutions Team

27

Avant Gard Hair Salon
HAIR: Shaun Settle
COLOR: Shaun Settle
MAKE-UP: Avant Gard Hair Salon Team
PHOTO: Scott Bryant
Art Direction by Larry Oskin
& The Marketing Solutions Team

Diadema Hair Fashion
HAIR: Diadema
MAKE-UP: 20100Milano
PHOTO: Stefano Bidini

Diadema Hair Fashion
HAIR: Diadema
MAKE-UP: 20100Milano
PHOTO: Stefano Bidini

Salon Coccolé
HAIR: Salon Coccolé
MAKE-UP: Salon Coccolé
PHOTO: Salon Coccolé

**John Amico Haircare & Jalyd Haircolor-
Petrosino's Parlor Salon**
HAIR: Ralph Petrosino
COLOR: Ralph Petrosino
MAKE-UP: Aimee Aviles
PHOTO: Scott Bryant
Art Direction by Larry Oskin
& The Marketing
Solutions Team

**John Amico Haircare
& Jalyd Haircolor**
HAIR: Yenz & Reinout Von Tilborg
COLOR: Yenz & Reinout Von Tilborg
MAKE-UP: Yenz & Reinout Von Tilborg
PHOTO: Scott Bryant
Art Direction by Larry Oskin
& The Marketing Solutions Team

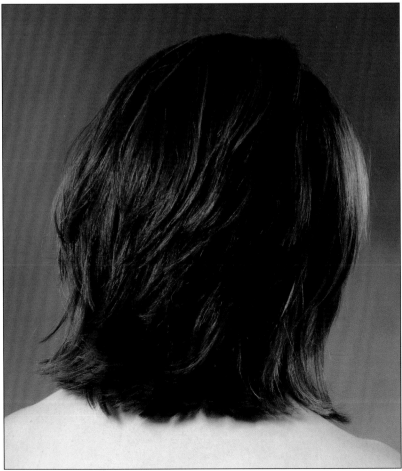

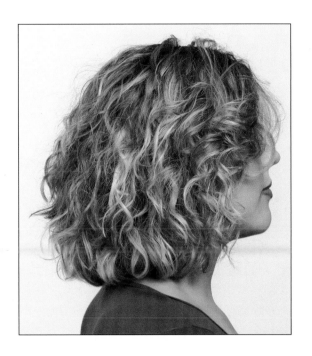

**John Amico Haircare &
Jalyd Haircolor-Studio Piazza Salon**
HAIR: Rene Mitsven
COLOR: Rene Mitsven
MAKE-UP: Rene Mitsven
PHOTO: Scott Bryant
Art Direction by Larry Oskin &
The Marketing Solutions Team

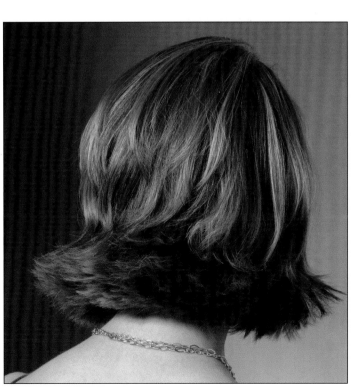

Alexander's Grand Salon & Spa
HAIR: Kathy Reddel
MAKE-UP: Katrina Halliwell
PHOTO: Taggart Winterhalter
for Purely Visual

Anu Salon and Spa
HAIR: Mado Nezry
MAKE-UP: Erique Lujan
PHOTO: Richard Viola

T.Carlton's Studio
HAIR: Christine DeStefano
MAKE-UP: T. Carlton's
PHOTO: Larry Hacken

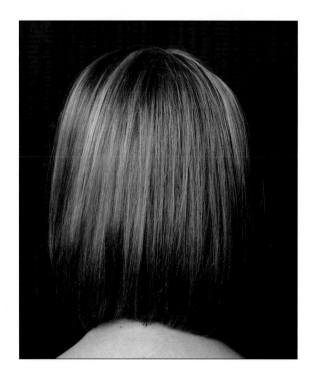

Alexander's Grand Salon & Spa
HAIR: Stacey Kriebel
MAKE-UP: Amy Kaniewski
PHOTO: Taggart Winterhalter
for Purely Visual

Crème Colour Lounge
HAIR: Valerie Braden
MAKE-UP: Jaime Queenin
PHOTO: Taggart Winterhalter
for Purely Visual

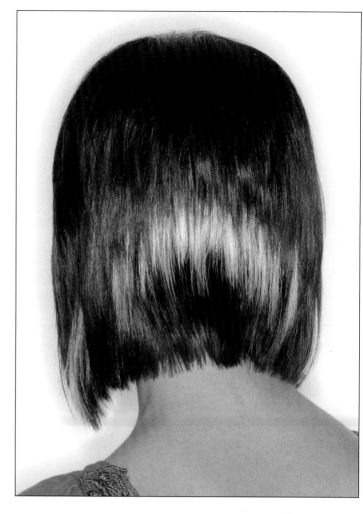

Tantrum Salon
HAIR: Shannon Trae Wedde
MAKE-UP: Jaime Queenin
PHOTO: Taggart Winterhalter
for Purely Visual

Salon Coccolé
HAIR: Salon Coccolé
MAKE-UP: Salon Coccolé
PHOTO: Salon Coccolé

**John Amico Haircare
& Jalyd Haircolor-
Petrosino's Parlor Salon**
HAIR: Ralph Petrosino
COLOR: Janine Kalahiki
MAKE-UP: Amie Miller
PHOTO: Scott Bryant
Art Direction by
Larry Oskin
& The Marketing
Solutions Team

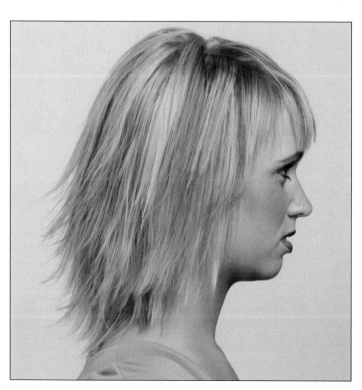

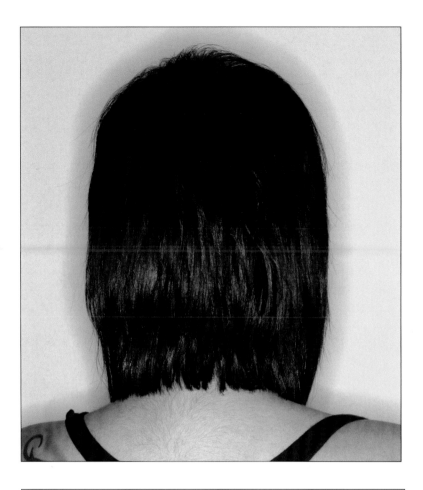

Tantrum Salon
HAIR: Hector Lopez
MAKE-UP: Jaime Queenin
PHOTO: Taggart Winterhalter
for Purely Visual

The Art of Hair Salon
HAIR: Michelle Whinna
MAKE-UP: Marcia Brazona
PHOTO:Ray Lansky

Tantrum Salon
HAIR: Hector Lopez
MAKE-UP: Jaime Queenin
PHOTO: Taggart Winterhalter
for Purely Visual

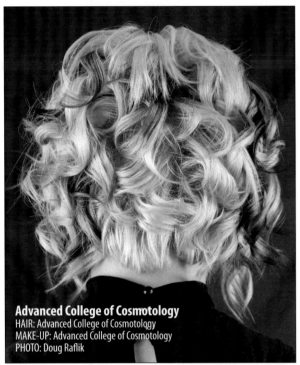

Advanced College of Cosmotology
HAIR: Advanced College of Cosmotology
MAKE-UP: Advanced College of Cosmotology
PHOTO: Doug Raflik

Mane Street
HAIR: Anne Nicole
PHOTO: Robert Holmes,
Shooting Stars

Shabangs Salon & Spa
HAIR: Samantha Ising
MAKE-UP: Maura Kofstad
PHOTO: Jim Fergusen

Diadema Hair Fashion
HAIR: Diadema
MAKE-UP: 20100Milano
PHOTO: Stefano Bidini

**John Amico Haircare
& Jalyd Haircolor-
Petrosino's Parlor Salon**
HAIR: Ralph Petrosino
COLOR: Aimee Aviles
MAKE-UP: Amie Miller
PHOTO: Scott Bryant
Art Direction by
Larry Oskin
& The Marketing
Solutions Team

O'Hair Salon & Spa
HAIR: Kerry Robertson
MAKE-UP: Jackie Hannan
PHOTO: Domenic Cicala

Sempre Bellezza
HAIR: Daniella DelFante
MAKE-UP: Jaime Queenin
PHOTO: Taggart Winterhalter
for Purely Visual

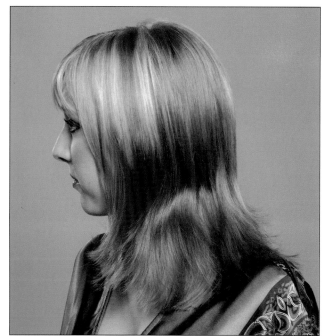

**Shabangs
Salon & Spa**
HAIR: Barbara Eberhart
MAKE-UP: Maura Kofstad
PHOTO: Jim Fergusen

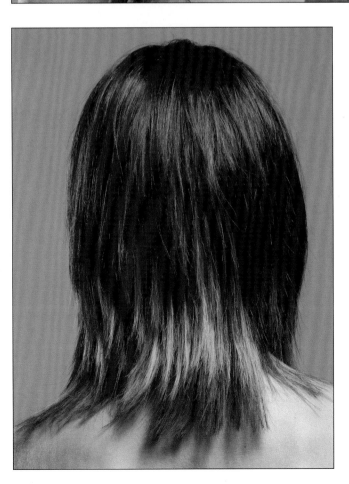

Avant Gard Hair Salon
HAIR: A.J. Williams
COLOR: A.J. Williams
MAKE-UP: Avant Gard
Hair Salon Team
PHOTO: Scott Bryant
Art Direction by
Larry Oskin
& The Marketing
Solutions Team

Diadema Hair Fashion
HAIR: Diadema
MAKE-UP: 20100Milano
PHOTO: Stefano Bidini

**So.Cap USA Hair Extensions-
Midwest/Octagon Spa & Salon**
HAIR: Vicki Millard
COLOR: Jancey Harty
EXTENSIONIST: Vicki Millard
MAKE-UP: Kira Auth
PHOTO: Scott Bryant
Art Direction by Larry Oskin
& The Marketing
Solutions Team

Hair Gallery
HAIR: Ginny Marone
PHOTO: Robert Holmes,
Shooting Stars

Edie's Styling Center-Oldsmar, FL
HAIR: Edie Noppenberger
COLOR: Edie Noppenberger
MAKE-UP: Nico
PHOTO: Scott Bryant
Art Direction by Larry Oskin
& The Marketing
Solutions Team

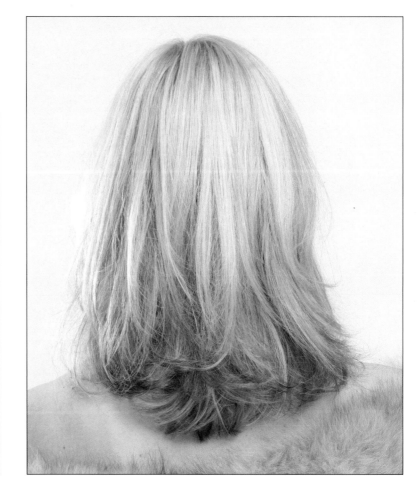

Intercoiffure Mondial
HAIR: Intercoiffure Artistic Team
MAKE-UP: Romualdo Piore
PHOTO: Claus Wickrath

LONG HAIR

T.Carlton's Studio
HAIR: Heather Darst
COLOR: Melissa Florek
PHOTO: Larry Hacken

T. Carlton's Studio
HAIR: Donna Pappas
MAKE-UP: T. Carlton's
PHOTO: Larry Hacken

American Hair
HAIR: Haley Kenyon
PHOTO: Robert Holmes,
Shooting Stars

Beauty Boutique
HAIR: Patsy Leaven
PHOTO: Robert Holmes,
Shooting Stars

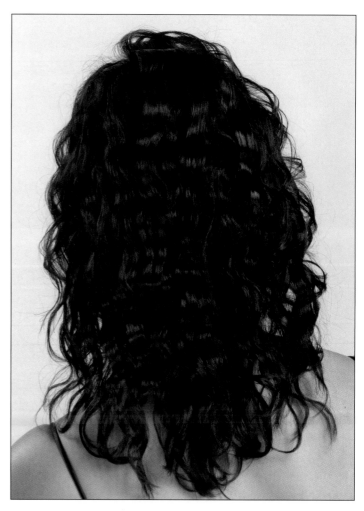

John Amico Haircare & Jalyd Haircolor-Salon By Michelle
HAIR: Michelle Little
COLOR: Michelle Little
MAKE-UP: Yenz Von Tilborg
PHOTO: Scott Bryant
Art Direction by
Larry Oskin &
The Marketing
Solutions Team

**Hair Benders Internationalé-
Chattanooga, TN**
HAIR: Hair Benders Design Team
COLOR: Hair Benders Design Team
MAKE-UP: Darin Wright
PHOTO: Scott Bryant
Art Direction by Larry Oskin &
The Marketing Solutions Team

élon Salon-Marietta, GA
HAIR: Emily Bruce
MAKE-UP: Fawn/Mac
PHOTO: Scott Bryant
Art Direction by
Larry Oskin &
The Marketing
Solutions Team

**Planet Salon-
Lexington, KY**
HAIR: Jason Parsons
PHOTO: Jeff Rogers

56

**John Amico Haircare
& Jalyd Haircolor-
Paula For You Salon**
HAIR: Sarah Interial
COLOR: Paula Boldman
MAKE-UP: Kirsten Kelly
PHOTO: Scott Bryant
Art Direction by
Larry Oskin
& The Marketing
Solutions Team

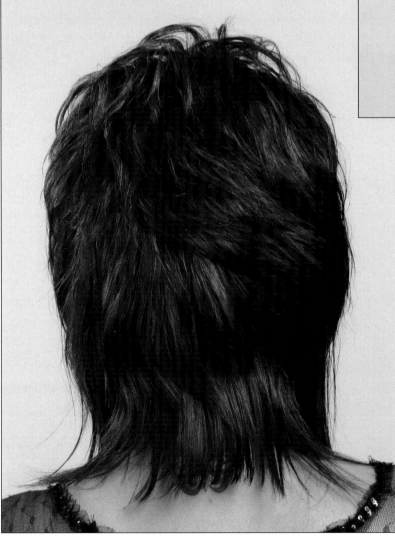

**Mitchell's Salons & Day Spas-
Cincinnati, Ohio**
HAIR: Vivian Moore
MAKE-UP: Lydia Brock
PHOTO: Annette McCall

58

**Indiana's Premier Hair Academy-
Indianapolis, IN**
HAIR: Melissa Fath
COLOR: Melissa Fath
MAKE-UP: Susan Stacy
PHOTO: Scott Bryant
Art Direction by Larry Oskin
& The Marketing
Solutions Team

**So.Cap USA Hair Extensions-
Midwest/Octagon Spa & Salon**
HAIR: Vicki Millard
COLOR & EXTENSIONIST: Vicki Millard
MAKE-UP: Kira Auth
PHOTO: Scott Bryant
Art Direction by Larry Oskin & The Marketing Solutions Team

Owen Wilson
PHOTO: Frederick M. Brown/
Getty Images

Diane Lane
PHOTO: Charley Gallay/
Getty Images

Evan Rachel Wood
PHOTO: Michael Loccisano/
Getty Images

Richard Gere
PHOTO: Mark Von Holden/Getty Images

60

Christina Ricci
PHOTO: Mark Davis/Getty Images

Taylor Swift
PHOTO: Scott Gries/Getty Images

Sammi Hanratty
PHOTO: Frederick M. Brown/Getty Images

Joseph Castanon
PHOTO: Michael Buckner/Getty Images

Madison Pettis
PHOTO: Frederick M. Brown/Getty Images

Marion Cotillard
PHOTO: Mike Marsland/Getty Images

Keith Urban
PHOTO: Bryan Bedder/Getty Images

Ryan Reynolds
PHOTO: Jim Spellman/Getty Images

Paula Abdul
PHOTO: Stephen Lovekin/Getty Images

Heidi Klum
PHOTO: John Shearer/
Getty Images

Nicole Kidman
PHOTO: Jon Kopaloff/Getty Images

Ryan Seacrest
PHOTO: Michael Tran/
Getty Images

Minka Kelly
PHOTO: Jon Kopaloff/Getty Images

Miley Cyrus
PHOTO: Stephen Shugarman/Getty Images

Carla Gugino
PHOTO:Stephen Shugarman/
Getty Images

Marion Cotillard
PHOTO: Steve Granitz/Getty Images

Amy Adams
PHOTO: Jeff Vespa/
Getty Images

LeAnn Rimes
PHOTO: Jon Kopaloff/
Getty Images

Joe Jonas
PHOTO: Jeffrey Meyer/Getty Images

Selena Gomez
PHOTO: Frederick M. Brown/
Getty Images

Chace Crawford
PHOTO: Scott Gries/Getty Images

Justin Timberlake
PHOTO: Kevin Winter/
Getty Images

Amanda Bynes
PHOTO: Michael Buckner/
Getty Images

Minka Kelly
PHOTO: Bryan Bedder/
Getty Images

Tobey Maguire
PHOTO: Francis Durand/
Getty Images

Aphodite Beauty Studio
HAIR: Janet Rakowia
PHOTO: Brian Morgan

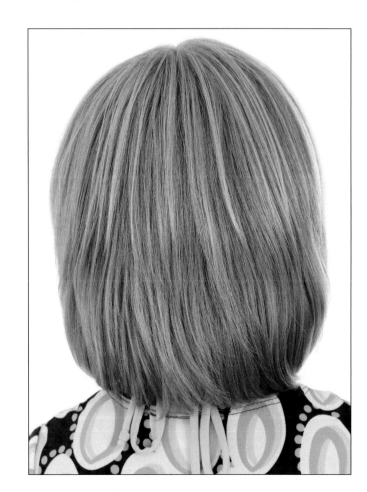

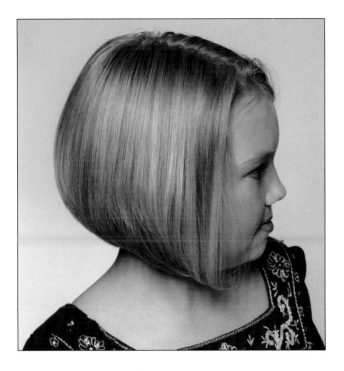

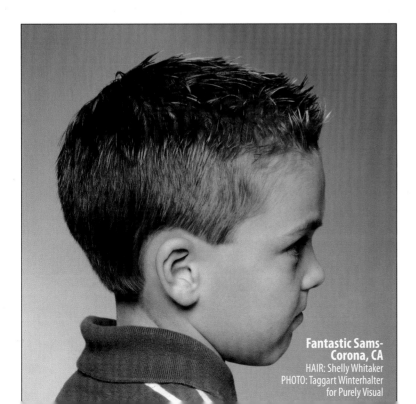

So.Cap USA Hair Extensions-Midwest/Octagon Spa & Salon
HAIR: Vicki Millard
COLOR: Vicki Millard
MAKE-UP: Kira Auth
PHOTO: Scott Bryant
Art Direction by Larry Oskin &
The Marketing Solutions Team

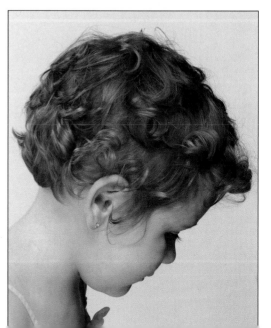

So.Cap USA Hair Extensions-Midwest/Octagon Spa & Salon
HAIR: Vicki Millard
COLOR: Vicki Millard
MAKE-UP: Kira Auth
PHOTO: Scott Bryant
Art Direction by Larry Oskin &
The Marketing Solutions Team

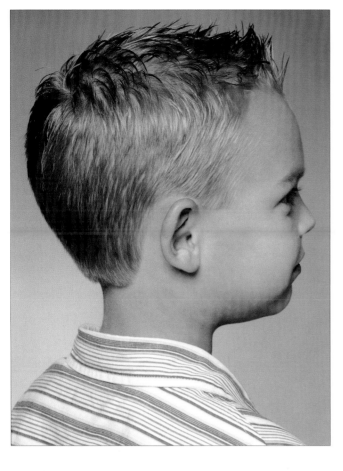

Fantastic Sams-Corona, CA
HAIR: Shelly Whitaker
PHOTO: Taggart Winterhalter
for Purely Visual

Sempre Bellezza
HAIR: Daniella DelFante
MAKE-UP: Jaime Queenin
PHOTO: Taggart Winterhalter
for Purely Visual

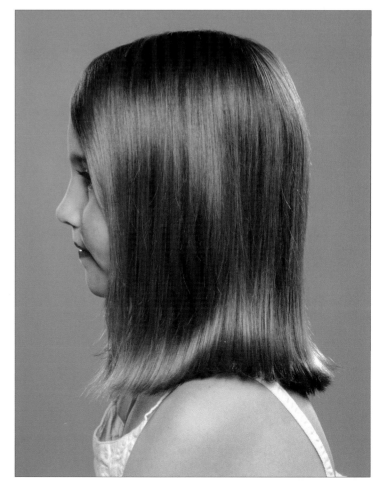

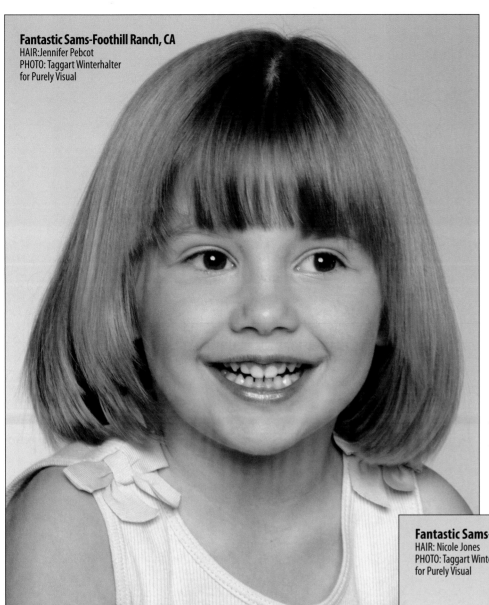

Fantastic Sams-Foothill Ranch, CA
HAIR: Jennifer Pebcot
PHOTO: Taggart Winterhalter
for Purely Visual

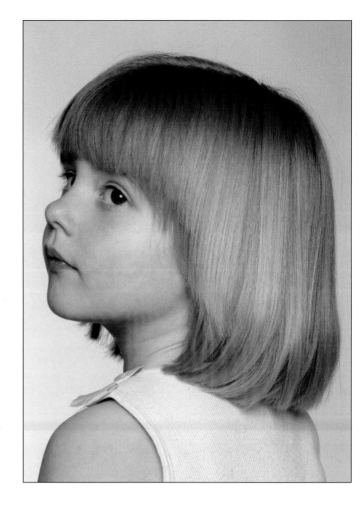

Fantastic Sams-Corona, CA
HAIR: Nicole Jones
PHOTO: Taggart Winterhalter
for Purely Visual

Fantastic Sams-Foothill Ranch, CA
HAIR: Charles Holdeman
PHOTO: Taggart Winterhalter
for Purely Visual

Fantastic Sams- Mira Loma, CA
HAIR: Magdalena Luevano
PHOTO: Taggart Winterhalter
for Purely Visual

73

Fantastic Sams-Corona, CA
HAIR: Shelly Whitaker
PHOTO: Taggart Winterhalter
for Purely Visual

**John Amico Haircare &
Jalyd Haircolor-David the Salon**
HAIR: Gina Blakey
COLOR: Gina Blakey
MAKE-UP: Gina Blakey
PHOTO: Scott Bryant
Art Direction by Larry Oskin
& The Marketing Solutions Team

Diadema Hair Fashion
HAIR: Diadema
PHOTO: Stefano Bidini

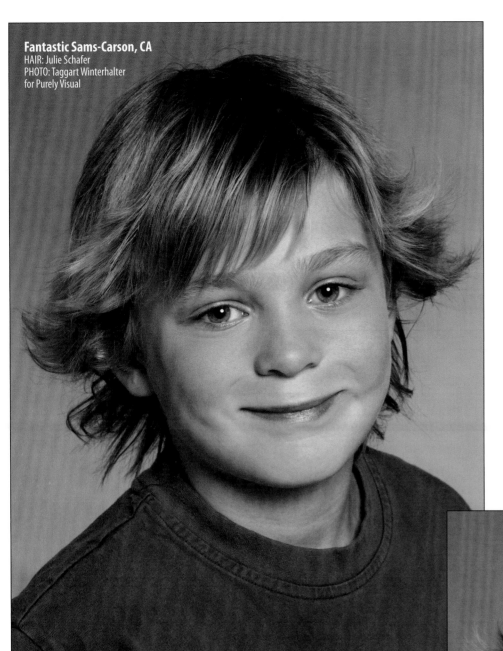

Fantastic Sams-Carson, CA
HAIR: Julie Schafer
PHOTO: Taggart Winterhalter
for Purely Visual

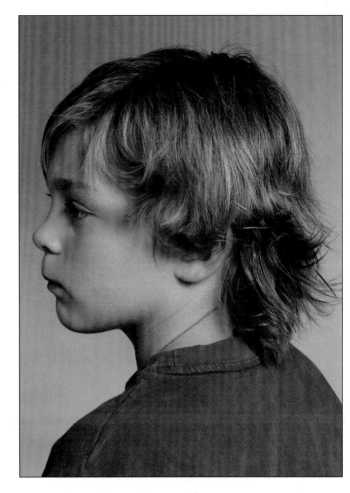

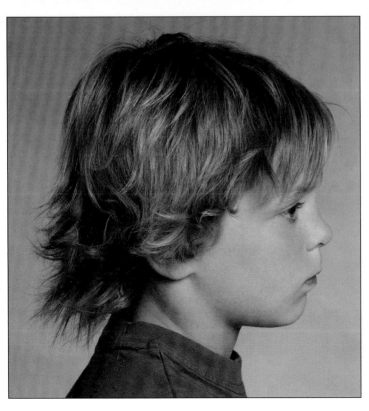

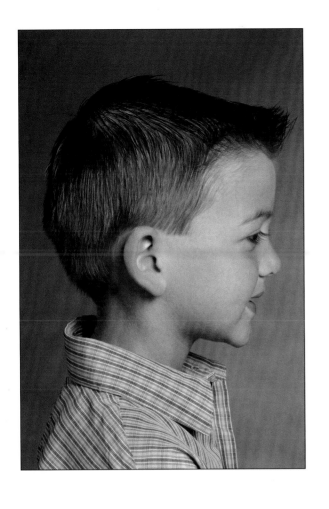

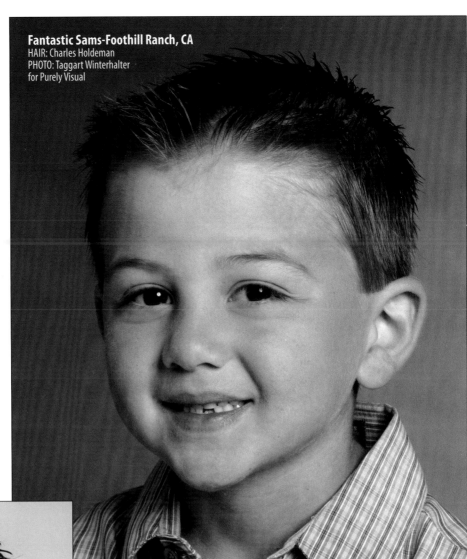

Fantastic Sams-Foothill Ranch, CA
HAIR: Charles Holdeman
PHOTO: Taggart Winterhalter
for Purely Visual

**Fantastic Sams-
Lake Elsinore, CA**
HAIR: Rosalia Gauna
PHOTO: Taggart Winterhalter
for Purely Visual

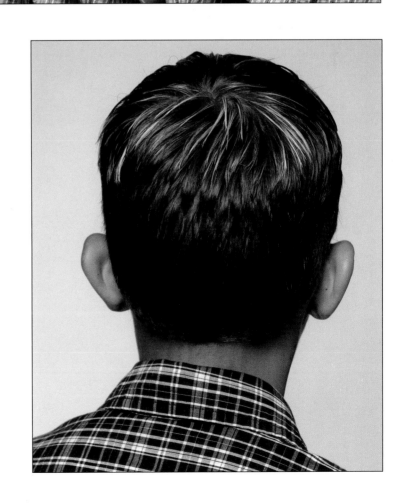

Advanced College of Cosmetology
HAIR: Advanced College of Cosmetology
MAKE-UP: Advanced College of Cosmetology
PHOTO: Doug Raflik Photography

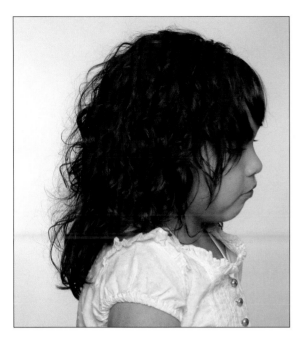

Fantastic Sams-Corona, CA
HAIR: Anna Reyes
PHOTO: Taggart Winterhalter
for Purely Visual

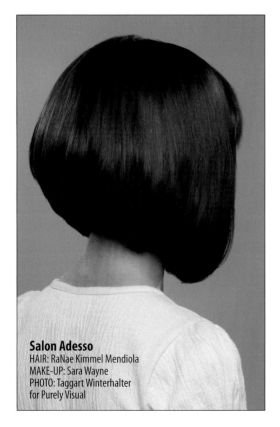

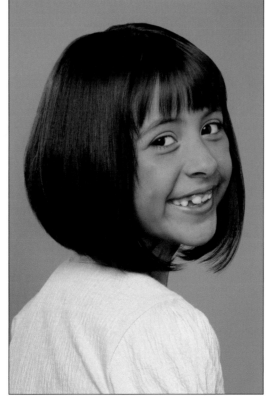

Salon Adesso
HAIR: RaNae Kimmel Mendiola
MAKE-UP: Sara Wayne
PHOTO: Taggart Winterhalter
for Purely Visual

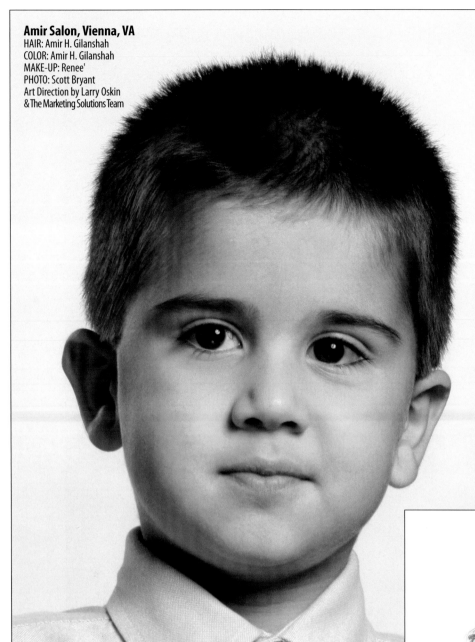

Amir Salon, Vienna, VA
HAIR: Amir H. Gilanshah
COLOR: Amir H. Gilanshah
MAKE-UP: Renee'
PHOTO: Scott Bryant
Art Direction by Larry Oskin
& The Marketing Solutions Team

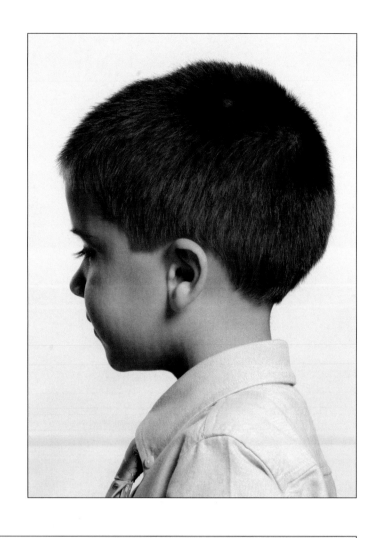

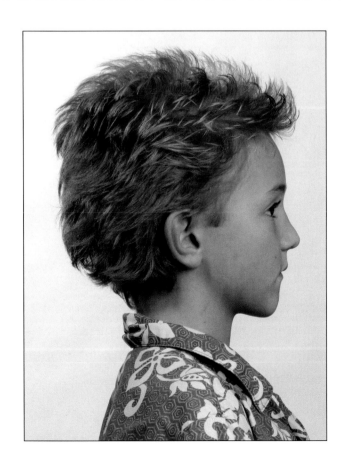

**John Amico Haircare &
Jalyd Haircolor-
New Yorker Salon,
Chicago, IL**
HAIR: John Zeman, Sr.
COLOR: John Zeman, Sr.
MAKE-UP: Marcella Vega
PHOTO: Scott Bryant
Art Direction by Larry Oskin
& The Marketing
Solutions Team

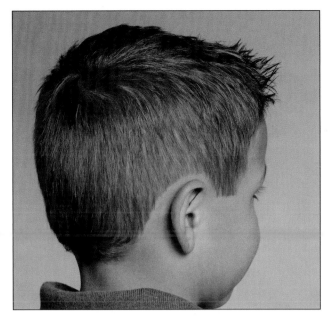

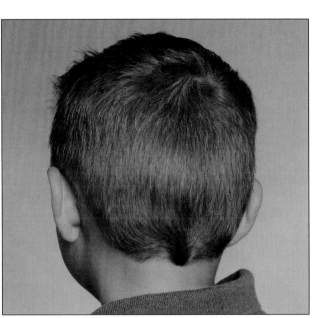

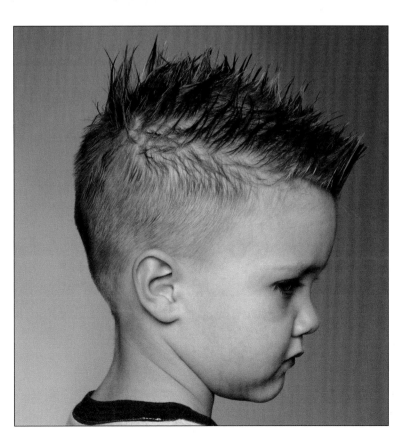

Diadema Hair Fashion
HAIR: X-men
MAKE-UP: Cristina Marzo per 20100Milano
PHOTO: Stefano Bidini

Fantastic Sams-Corona. CA
HAIR: Shelly Whitaker
PHOTO: Taggart Winterhalter for Purely Visual

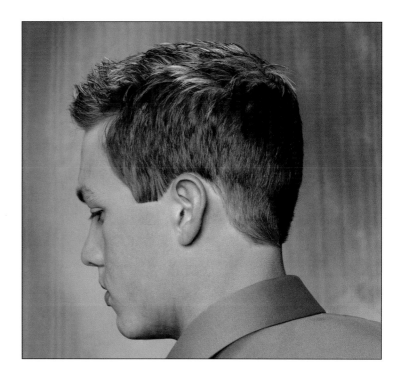

Diadema Hair Fashion
HAIR: X-men
MAKE-UP: Cristina Marzo per 20100Milano
PHOTO: Stefano Bidini

Pivot Point International
HAIR: Jen Hagenmuller-Pivot Point Germany
MAKE-UP: Lori Neapolitan
PHOTO: Nathan Becker/David Placek

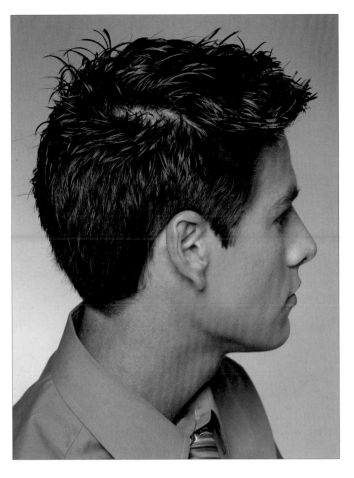

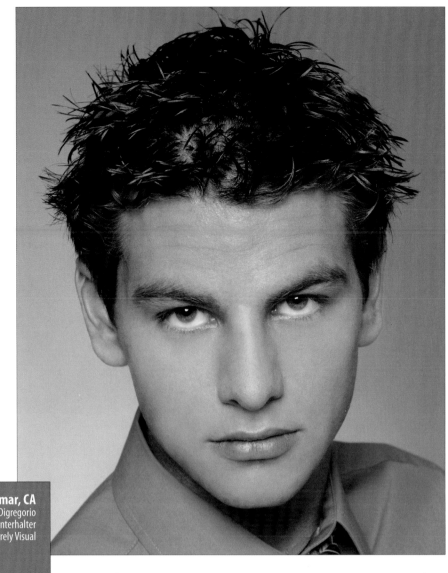

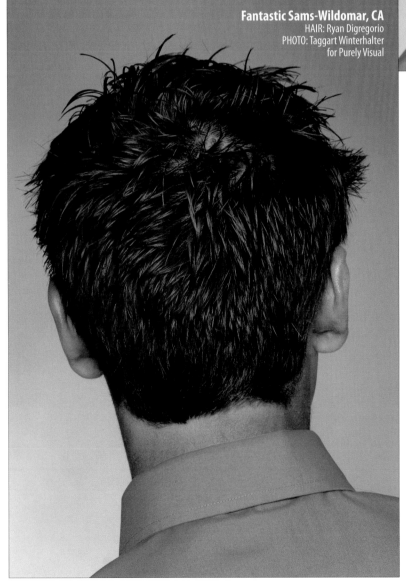

Fantastic Sams-Wildomar, CA
HAIR: Ryan Digregorio
PHOTO: Taggart Winterhalter
for Purely Visual

Coiffeur XYZ Createur
HAIR: Michael Del Bronco for XYZ
COLOR: Sylvie Hendrikx et Maryline Forges
MAKE-UP: Juan Pacifico
PHOTO: Evelyne De Mey
@BG project

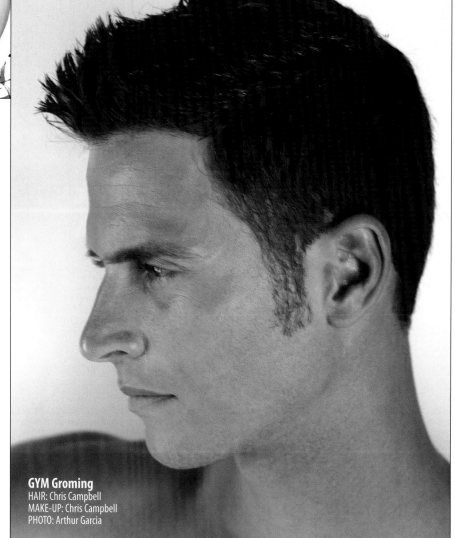

GYM Groming
HAIR: Chris Campbell
MAKE-UP: Chris Campbell
PHOTO: Arthur Garcia

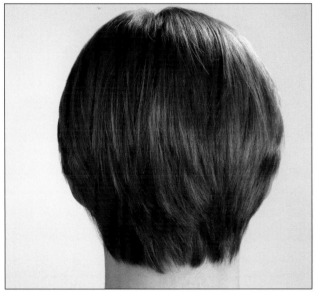

Planet Salon-Beverly Hills, CA
HAIR: Geno Chapman
MAKE-UP: Michelle Tabor
PHOTO: Michael Block

**John Amico
Haircare &
Jalyd
Haircolor-
The New Yorker
Hair Design-
Chicago**
HAIR: John Zeman, Sr.
COLOR: John Zeman, Sr.
MAKE-UP: Brandy Long
PHOTO: Scott Bryant
Art Direction by Larry Oskin &
The Marketing Solutions Team

**John Amico Haircare &
Jalyd Haircolor-
Top Reviews Salon,
Plainfield, IL**
HAIR: Lynn Villiaros
COLOR: Lynn Villiaros
MAKE-UP: Malia E. Villiaros
PHOTO: Scott Bryant
Art Direction by Larry Oskin
& The Marketing
Solutions Team

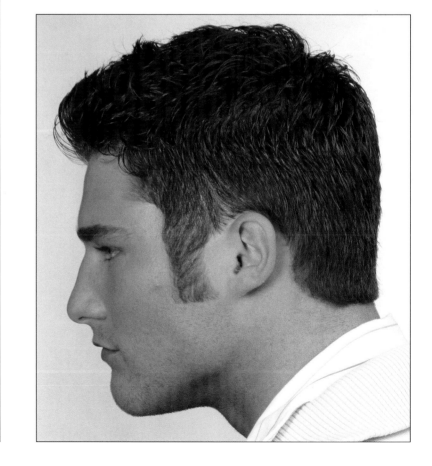

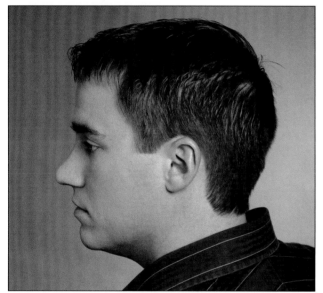

Fantastic Sams-Foothill Ranch, CA
HAIR: Charles Holdeman
PHOTO: Taggart Winterhalter for Purely Visual

**Planet Salon-
Beverly Hills, CA**
HAIR: Geno Chapman
MAKE-UP: Michelle Tabor
PHOTO: Michael Block

89

**John Amico Haircare & Jalyd Haircolor-
The New Yorker Salon**
HAIR: John Zeman, Sr.
COLOR: John Zeman, Sr.
MAKE-UP: Yenz &
Reinout Von Tilborg
PHOTO: Scott Bryant
Art Direction by
Larry Oskin
& The Marketing
Solutions Team

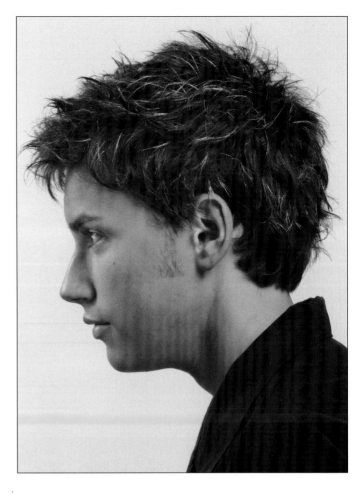

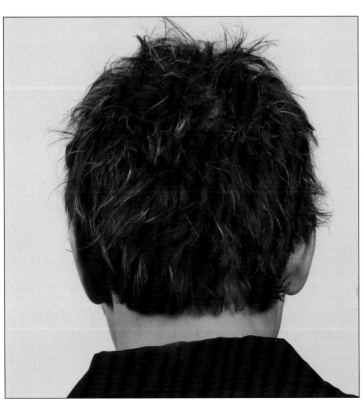

Diadema Hair Fashion
HAIR: Diadema
MAKE-UP: 20100Milano
PHOTO: Stefano Bidini

Salon Coccolé
HAIR: Salon Coccolé
MAKE-UP: Salon Coccolé
PHOTO: Salon Coccolé

Pivot Point International
HAIR: Simone Muterle, Pivot Point Italy
MAKE-UP: Dino
PHOTO: Mike van den Toom/David Placek

Advanced College of Cosmetology
HAIR: Advanced College of Cosmetology
MAKE-UP: Advanced College of Cosmetology
PHOTO: Doug Raflik Photography

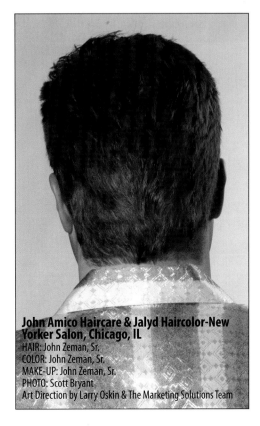

John Amico Haircare & Jalyd Haircolor-New Yorker Salon, Chicago, IL
HAIR: John Zeman, Sr.
COLOR: John Zeman, Sr.
MAKE-UP: John Zeman, Sr.
PHOTO: Scott Bryant
Art Direction by Larry Oskin & The Marketing Solutions Team

Crème Colour Lounge
HAIR: Briana Naylor
MAKE-UP: Jaime Queenin
PHOTO: Taggart Winterhalter
for Purely Visual

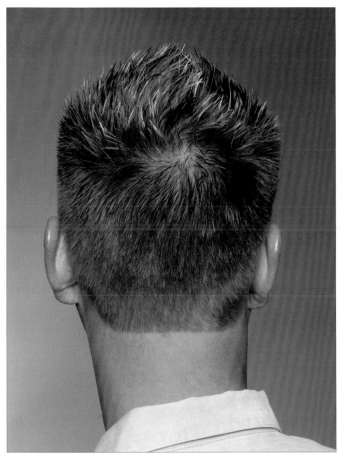

**Fantastic Sams-
Lake Elsinore, CA**
HAIR: Rosalia Gauna
PHOTO: Taggart Winterhalter
for Purely Visual

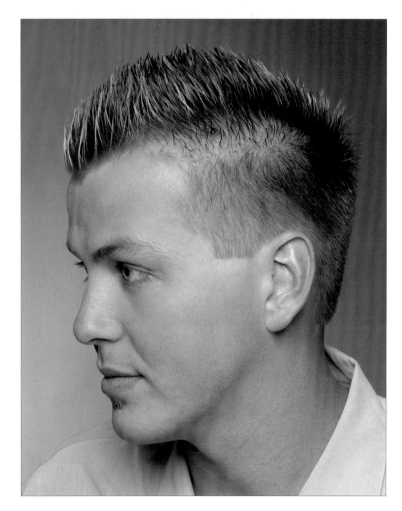

MEN'S HAIR

95

Planet Salon-Beverly Hills, CA
HAIR: Geno Chapman
MAKE-UP: Michelle Tabor
PHOTO: Michael Block

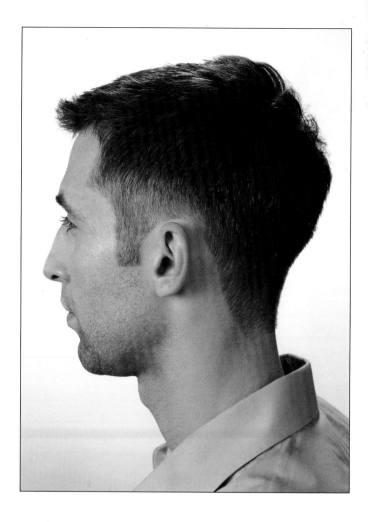

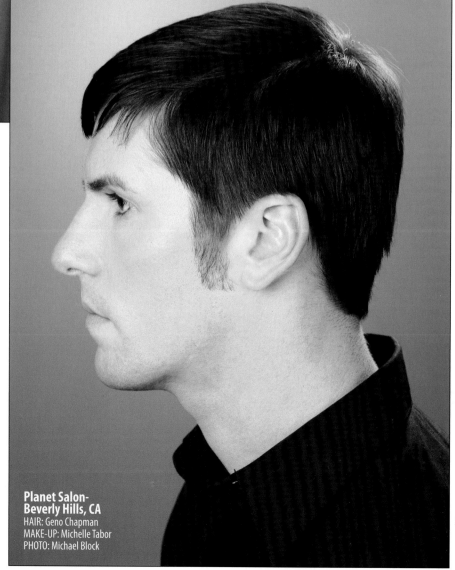

**Planet Salon-
Beverly Hills, CA**
HAIR: Geno Chapman
MAKE-UP: Michelle Tabor
PHOTO: Michael Block

Publisher/CEO: Deborah Carver • Managing Director: Sheryl Lenzkes • Art Director: Michael Block • Photo Coordinator: Mara Soldinger
To Contact Us: Creative Age Communications • 7628 Densmore Avenue, Van Nuys, California 91406-2042 • PH 800.634.8500 • FAX 818.782.7450